DEAL

ALSO BY RANDALL MANN

POETRY

A Better Life

Proprietary

Straight Razor

Breakfast with Thom Gunn

Complaint in the Garden

CRITICISM

The Illusion of Intimacy: On Poetry

DEAL

NEW AND SELECTED POEMS

RANDALL MANN

COPPER CANYON PRESS

PORT TOWNSEND, WASHINGTON

Cover design: Phil Kovacevich

Sections of selected poems from *Deal* first appeared in the following volumes:

Straight Razor, copyright © 2013 by Randall Mann. Reprinted by permission of the publisher, Persea Books, Inc. (New York), www.perseabooks.com. All rights reserved.

Proprietary, copyright © 2017 by Randall Mann. Reprinted by permission of the publisher, Persea Books, Inc. (New York), www.perseabooks.com. All rights reserved.

A Better Life, copyright © 2021 by Randall Mann. Reprinted by permission of the publisher, Persea Books, Inc. (New York), www.perseabooks.com. All rights reserved.

Copper Canyon Press is in residence at Fort Worden State Park in Port Townsend, Washington, under the auspices of Centrum. Centrum is a gathering place for artists and creative thinkers from around the world, students of all ages and backgrounds, and audiences seeking extraordinary cultural enrichment.

LIBRARY OF CONGRESS CATALOGING-IN-PUBLICATION DATA
Names: Mann, Randall, author.
Title: Deal : new and selected poems / Randall Mann.
Description: Port Townsend, Washington : Copper Canyon Press, 2023. |
    Summary: "A collection of poetry by Randall Mann"—Provided by
    publisher.
Identifiers: LCCN 2022050131 (print) | LCCN 2022050132 (ebook) |
    ISBN 9781556596766 (paperback) | ISBN 9781619322769 (epub)
Subjects: LCGFT: Poetry.
Classification: LCC PS3613.A55 D43 2023 (print) | LCC PS3613.A55 (ebook) |
    DDC 811/.6—dc23/eng/20221123
LC record available at https://lccn.loc.gov/2022050131
LC ebook record available at https://lccn.loc.gov/2022050132

9 8 7 6 5 4 3 2 FIRST PRINTING

COPPER CANYON PRESS
Post Office Box 271
Port Townsend, Washington 98368
www.coppercanyonpress.org

Acknowledgments

Grateful acknowledgment is made to the editors of the following publications where the new poems, often in slightly different form, first appeared:

The Adroit Journal: "September," "The Turn of the Year," "A Walk in the Park"

Air/Light: "Containment," "In the Beginning," "Poem Beginning with a Line by Wayne Koestenbaum," "The Scene"

The Arkansas International: "Days"

Copper Nickel: "Deal"

The Cortland Review: "The Summer of 1996"

fourteen poems: "One-Night Stand"

jubilat: "Wi-Fi"

MumberMag: "Luck," "A Step Past Disco"

Narrative: "Friday," "The Past"

Oversound: "Tagged"

The Paris Review: "In the Rapid Autumn of Libraries"

Quarterly West: "Blue"

The Sewanee Review: "Against Metaphor," "Double Life"

Grateful acknowledgment also to Persea Books, Inc. who supported the publication of the following volumes from which are reprinted sections of this collection: *Straight Razor, Proprietary,* and *A Better Life.*

Thank you to Miguel Murphy, the first reader of my poems. Thanks also to Geoffrey Brock, Debora Greger, Wayne Miller, Michael Nott, Sabina Piersol, D.A. Powell, Atsuro Riley, Aaron Smith, Eric Smith, Susan Steinberg, and Sidney Wade.

In memory: Michelle Boisseau, Richard Howard, and Kevin Killian.

Thank you to my editor, Michael Wiegers, for his faith in my work, and to the entire Copper Canyon team.

for my parents

&

Miguel Murphy

CONTENTS

New Poems

from *Complaint in the Garden* (2004)

from *Breakfast with Thom Gunn* (2009)

from *Straight Razor* (2013)

from *Proprietary* (2017)

from *A Better Life* (2021)

DEAL

New Poems

I dread the color of the answer Yes.

Bill Knott

A Walk in the Park

The palms along
Dolores Street
do not belong.
The past looms
like chat rooms.

At the top
of the park,
a fellow
suns himself.
(They call the hill

the *fruit shelf*.)
The view
from here
ruthless—
more or less.

We play a game
of name
the building
that was razed.
Ding, ding.

Downtown
off-limits
as a wish,
or noun.
The weeds

like all the right
wrong words.
Or none.
Swish, swish.
I'd trade

interest rate
and day-trade
for clean-
your-house-
in-the-nude days,

and date-the-broke-
actor days.
Urinal talk:
this is as close
as we can get.

Show don't show,
and yet, and yet—
the city
part sunny
aggression,

part accent piece.
Rush, rush.
The smoke;
the dirt;
the sky—

I spy
the gospel
in the park,
septic,
lush as real money.

In the Beginning

I am sorry. I am sorry. But I am gone.
Laura Jensen

There was a man.
Who spun saccharine
turns of phrase,
burns on the lips.
A lapse in judgment
occurred, he half
inferred. Never meant.

Who peeled ailments
off pill bottles
on a shelf,
swallowed
more than allowed,
to show safety.
Because it was safe,

he slaked his thirst
with ache—but not
at first. The cause,
a stiff knot. He gifted
a scarf with strings—
Whatever you say,
he sings—and some new

little boots.
Like *Caligula* (1979)—
stiff upper art;
Penthouse Pets—
he gets it both ways.
Monstrous and hurt,
another Robert Lowell.

A man is the owl
on the clock
in the corner.
A man of the house
for sale by owner.
In other words,
lay down

your flesh cards.
A man is clues,
broken news.
In the beginning,
a man is sewage.
And the beginning
is always.

Deal

The sun sets.
We are all robots.
Market forces.

Ed Smith

Eating cereal
over the sink,
I think,
this is
what's real:
the urgent
piss;
the grout
like doubt.
By now,
Anonymous,
no
gent,
is in
his Lyft . . .

Adrift.
This fall,
all
the kids
want
to shoot
vids,
amateur
auteurs,
little
hard
Godards.
To boot.
Spittle,
my haunt.

I want
my hair.
And,
a split,
somewhere
between
mathematics
and tricks
buried
in the yard,
the dream
a multilevel
scheme.
Get
a shovel.

I shrivel—
by
bleak
acronym,
boutique
gym,
Commie
leak,
Jimmy
hats,
metallic
antibiotic,
lost
chats
on a hill.

A hell
of
passive
investors.
Reboot
love,
with massive

clawback
provisions,
money
dripping off
your robot
back.
The monsters.
My stars.

Blue

My parents hid
a loopy vid
on the shelf,

The Honey Cup
with Sonny Landham:
my massive ham;

my upshot.
(Years later,
he put on clothes,

starred in *Predator,*
and ran for KY
senator.)

Sonny stroked
with care
his feathered hair.

I inserted my-
self.
What I wanted:

to cruise
the Live Oaks mall—
swill, stall,

glorious hole—
stuck in the back
bookstore rack,

my *Blueboy* tucked
behind *Sporting News,*
and the torn-

out waxed
bodies—
dead now,

beautiful then.
And then?
We know what then.

We think,
we cannot bear to think,
we do.

The Summer of 1996

The librarian,
my grave
purveyor
of white

gloves,
rare books:
King Payne
allegedly

danced
on a white
horse;
King Charles IX

named
the peninsula
New France,
off chance,

in 1564.
That's Florida
for you!
Right.

A summer
of kings,
and clubs,
and queens:

the late
Todd aka
Toddonna
(for money,

she feigned
only
Madonna)
crawled

onto the scene—
drag fight;
fag night—
at Ambush.

Butch.
A monocle
dangled
in her razored

neckline;
she saw us all
for what
we were—

not a lick.
Sick
of suspect
looks,

of plague,
I walked
Paynes Prairie:
one more

vague
elegy,
one more
basin

gone dry,
sand,
fairy
dust . . .

—A heron
stood rigid
as a palace
guard,

great
and blue
and useless.
The last word.

A Step Past Disco

I took a step
past disco.
Could still
discern
the strings,

the horn,
like a burn
slow to heal.
Infectious,
the hook

already
curled
in the body
like a comma,
or a buddy.

I took.
I clicked/
unclicked,
hope
a velvet rope.

Disco:
Lyrics
either
for just
one night

or *love*
for life—
no in between.
The drama.
I am

between,
young enough
not to have
lost
all my friends,

old enough
to have felt
(I feel)
any moment
the ferryman

will visit.
Rock
the boat,
don't rock
the boat.

Disco,
I took a step.
It's been
years.
Of forcing

functions,
token
liberation,
coercing
conjunctions,

and stroking
myself,
the celluloid
dead
my valuation.

A void.
Men come,
disposable
as thumbs,
opposable

as income.
The ones
I met
a data set
of none.

Nay, nay,
Fluffy,
they used
to say.
Who are

they?
Crooked
lashes,
side eye
like a dash—

broken
wishes—
the dance,
the outline
of religion,

and splashes
of Jean Naté
choking the air.
Fragments,
like errors,

the distance.

In the Rapid Autumn of Libraries

how softly one is seduced by whispers.
Take notice, when leafing through, say, a Calvino novel,
of all the pages gone blank

(this is the end
of letters); the social insects, like ants
on the windowsill: feel the corpses hardened.

In the distance, the Golden Gate—vultures riding a thermal
in the distance. The Golden Gate vultures riding a thermal:
on the windowsill, feel the corpses, hardened,

of letters, the social insects, like ants.
This is the end.
Of all the pages gone blank,

take notice: when leafing through, say, "A Calvino novel."
How? Softly. One is seduced by whispers
in the rapid autumn of libraries.

Days

Because no
transaction
is repugnant,

I look
at the moon.
I look up

this moon,
called a *fish moon*.
It is perfect

if I don't arrange for
metaphor. I do,
like an awkward

transition to talk.
My philosophy
hollow

as a list,
or formalist.
I swallow

the word
empathy,
then *awe*.

(Must be
angling
for sympathy.)

Metallic
as a phallic
age

to go.
Don't go.
That hiss

in the ear?
Near-
miss;

dissonance.
Indrawn,
like a long con,

a marriage.
The yards,
medicated.

I take a nap:
shoegaze.
Chin up?

Days.
I myself am hell
if I know.

Go on, spoof
me with proof.
The least

I deserve.
This life apart
is clip art.

Wi-Fi

after Karl Tierney

It's Tuesday inside,
and I'm thick.
Half microplastic,
half *giallo* flick.

My work,
nominal
data in the lap,
a lake

or dance.
Make it clap.
Does that make
sense,

like a disingenuous
question?
Anecdotal,
beige

as the Fed book?
Not at all.
Not only
is it 6 months

past my birthday,
but I'm 48
and *nice job*
don't look my age.

I try to list
what I have missed:
hobnob,
and the knee-jerk

comparison
to a domestic
animal,
one-trick.

I tease
a trade,
a scrape.
I hum along

a nineties
song:
*Don't walk
away* by Jade;

*You're my little
secret,* Xscape.
A paper bill
(I overheard)

has been
canceled,
like a word,
or man.

Sold.
Such fun,
which one.
I've had my fill.

The Past

For this year's Pride, we're asked to stay inside.
To reconsider gay, old times: the die-ins;

the clocked queens who threw coins
at blue shirts. Icons!

And subtle cuts a part of speech, no question:
One dims one's light, one quits

that job and heads to the trough
for warm solace. We had to go, hurt

the ones we loved, *past tense*—the anger
is gratifying, mostly, out of range . . .

—It's hard to say when this will end, so try.
The fog through slats unfolds like a story.

Double Life

Let's go
to Ocean Beach
to undermine
the line:

vultures flick
arithmetic;
pups dart,
all heart.

It's grief,
capsized,
an itch
of otherwise.

The wind
elides—
relief
a thief—

the double life
of consonants:
passing; running.
Theatrical

as the clap
of a laptop,
no one careful
does that. Careful.

Our makeup
sand,
which arranges
and repeats

itself
to protect
itself,
like CRISPR.

A stat
whisper:
Why
do snaps

numb
rather than
enhance?
Light

oversexed
yet sexless,
more edge
than gape,

or gag.
Can, oh,
anyone
be impolite

before night?
Let's do it.
Let's fall
into fear

like the veneer
grin
and weak
chin

of a
beloved
dictator.
Roll

in rash,
stud
in flesh.
You can

try
to relax.
But it's later
than syntax.

Luck

The daily spray
of Castro Street
gaily washes away
indiscreet flushes

before I wake.
Not sure how
I am now.
I pull the shade,

my shadow
my train.
Luck, this much
is plain:

hatchet face,
ratchet grin.
The bin
needs emptying

again—
too little.
It's true, I'm in
the middle

of life, so what.
No myth,
only math.
I'm just glad

I have enough
change
for laundry,
and August mist

is giving way
to a single ray
of sun.
What else is there

but comparison?
A poem
is staged
like home;

sunk,
like cost;
a ladder
like the color *yes.*

When I was drunk,
I fell engaged
to a grad stud—
pilsner, sneer,

gray matter,
molly—
melancholy
as the Cocteau Twins:

Stay and stay
and fail and fail.
I did and did.
You know a man.

—And then one day,
I had to pay
for might-have-beens.
I think I can. I can.

The check is in the mail.

September

for D.A. Powell

The birds
are relentless. Oh?
Well, the unseen,
maybe they've always

been this loud.
Yes and no,
like always,
beyond words . . .

Here's one: *death*.
A classic. Death
is all the little hints—
a blown porch light,

screeches
and raccoon prints
on the back steps—
then nothing

in the morning,
that after-party.
When it's all right.
I've seen a lot

of free porn
and speeches,
but California
is on fire

so let me shut
the actual door.
At least
my recent

trip to the clinic
was uneventful—
thanks, pandemic—
not like in April

when I peed
in a cup, etc.,
and was told I was stuck
with four STDs.

Four! Not exactly
a shock.
I worry
about my small

bladder;
I tell myself
it's always
been like this—

it has—
but I guess
it's getting worse:
I never sleep

through the night,
and my nightmare
is not getting
assigned the aisle

on a flight. Oh,
to travel again!
Cars still
are barreling

over the top
of Castro;
someone's
going somewhere.

On a day
the weather index
is green,
Doug and I meet

in the park.
He hands me
tomatoes
in a Cole Hardware

bag and unwraps
his newest penis
painting—such care
with the pubic hair!—

and we read aloud
new poems
at the Music
Concourse,

then order dipped
soft serve
at the Twirl and Dip
behind the music . . .

Of course,
there is no music
anymore.
We simply devour

what is ours.

Containment

November 2018

This is an attempt
to contain a wildfire.
Mistakes will be repeated:
look elsewhere for measure.

To contain a wildfire,
against myth,
look elsewhere. For measure,
remains are a number

against myth:
counts of manslaughter.
Remains are a number
set forth by Pacific Gas and Electric.

Counts of manslaughter,
aka, Camp Fire.
Set forth by Pacific Gas and Electric
a *liability,*

aka, Camp Fire.
It isn't easy to see
a liability.
Ash falls upon us all.

It isn't easy to see.
This is an attempt.
Ash falls upon us: All
mistakes will be repeated.

One-Night Stand

No one is ever innocent.

David Trinidad

Not quite.
A few unruly
hours at most, our

feverish messages
a diary of desire—
wait,

can we still *desire*
in a poem? You're
so nineties,

my inner critic says.
Also, show
us dick.

Who has time
for the night,
what with internal

breed and rhyme.
Drink the fifth.
The heart's

merch?
I have to say
you wear it well. Well,

commitment's
overrated—
but no one rates.

Or sleeps over,
much. So much over-
compensation,

a contributor's
note. A visitor's
throat. The to-do list

too grand, bland
as fortune. Taken
on the chin, idiom.

Like language, age
abbreviated,
I luv u thrust

into fetish:
a lash, a bushel
and a peck.

Crucial that you
choke my neck.
I care only

on days ending in why,
a joke. Not fair:
I want to feel dumb

as a box of hair,
numb as air hanging
there, shoes on a wire . . .

I've lost
what I need to lose.
Now look at the time:

how has it been
two years
since David

brought me to
Chicago?
I stayed

in a cavernous
suite in the dorms;
I had to

physically
sign in my tricks
in front of the

security guard (sorry
David). The pho
was spectacular

at that one
place we tried,
twice, though.

David
is so nice,
and mysterious,

a great underrated
poet! I didn't
tell him exactly that,

but we commiserated
on Sexton,
and booze,

and how much
we like this life
alone.

David.
When I said
sorry:

I'm not sorry.

The Scene

1

I weigh in
like a boxer.
I prompt.
A split lip
of simile;
a formality.

Then say
done and done,
post-money—
redundancy
the poverty,
the tea

closer
to role-play.
Disparity,
what pulls
away:
American

money!
So green
and dull—
but as we all
know,
dullness wins,

eventually.
One nation
of hydration,
bluffs,
and rotator
cuffs . . .

2

Later,
my slightly
younger
neighbor
will come
over,

in character
and shorts.
He calls me
Coach—
the scene—
reveals a patch

of itch
under his jock.
I'm no fool.
Ketoconazole,
we'll never
break.

A performance
where every
nobody wins,
mild-
to-regret
my statuette.

It isn't even
all that fun.
(Fun ends
when
you let
them in.)

3

Men like us
are forever
grieving.
Loss
isn't loss,
it's a limited series:

episode 1,
sequins;
2,
a bruise;
number you
know the rest.

Garishly shot,
like never.
I have
a small
window.
It's not bird

time yet, but
it is bird weather.
My wingspan
cuddlesome
(gross).
And my own

special
motiveless
malignity. Dignity,
I'm here
for fun
and friends.

4

Near beer,
tight ends.
Night bends.
I know
it's late
for a love game.

Which isn't
sadness,
or freedom,
it's a feeling
that precedes
feeling, a narcotic

urge of mythic
injury.
I'm a coach
without advice.
The balm?
Go on.

Tagged

in memory of Kevin Killian

The flowers never wilt.
The gallerist, a brute.
Kevin flips his phone
into a crystal flute.

We order pay-per-view,
a short by Kenneth Anger.
I doff my undershirt
and eye a wire hanger.

I'll see him by the cache.
I'll do as I am told.
And when he frames, I freeze—
the center cannot fold.

The sheet is haute couture.
He wears the latest taste.
The choker, little pearls—
like us, he says, of paste.

Friday

Is this a story
or a problem,
a colleague said.
I'm dead!
Which is to say,

living
for her shade.
I switch off
my face,
and chat,

Sorry.
Having
issues
Anything
but that . . .

I'm looking
to stream.
I settle on
I Killed My Mother.
Rotten Tomatoes'

pithy
description?
"A young homosexual
has problems
with his mother,"

which is also
every film ever
when I watch.
The first film
I ever saw

was *Citizen Kane,*
nice start but also
are you kidding,
a lesson
in all-

downhill-
from-here—
it was at the
Kentucky
Theatre,

a palace
with delicious
Orange Whip.
I was six.
The first

gay thing
I remember
other than
the longing
was seeing

Rock Hudson
on a stretcher
on the news.
I didn't know
I knew . . .

*Have a great
weekend,*
we end
our e-mails,
late in the day.

Great.
Like the
weekend,

modifiers
have a way

of taking us
farther
away:
the long
walk;

the afternoon
read.
Regret.
Marooned
on my shelves,

like Paul
Monette.
All
my ambitious
friends want

to talk about
is joy.
Oh boy:
The End.
Maybe that's

fine,
maybe satire—
so much rolls
off the tongue.
There is always

the distance
to revise.
Look how
I'm undoing
my own ruin

now.

Poem Beginning with a Line by Wayne Koestenbaum

Airports are gay bars in denial.
Look at how I saunter in:
gripping my name-brand totes
(behind the security rope,
the handsy agent);

proving I am myself.
The slow walk, where somebodies see me.
The sidling up to the bar to kill time.
The obsession: uniforms.
The repetition of the word *terminal*.

The repetition of the word *terminal*—
the obsession. Uniforms
sidling up to the bar to kill, Time
the slow walk where some bodies see me
proving I am, myself.

The handsy agent
behind the security rope:
gripping. My name brand? Totes
look at how I saunter in . . .
Airports are gay. Bars, in denial.

Against Metaphor

Gold is your friend
But gold starves you
Alfred Starr Hamilton

It's absurd,
how famished.
The fast fashion
of ghastly
lit fame
a golden age of—
Never mind.
The truth is
I've had minor
abstraction surgery,
can you tell.
Limits ago,
the go-go boy
in my bubble

overfilled
my receptacle,
so we traipsed out
to rue de Fleurus,
Operation
Stealth Poubelle. Hell,
say the word *go*
once, and he will—
nothing gold can. Say
go twice
and add a *boy*,
he'll stay if coins fly
into a pool of drool.
Speaking of:

it's Thursday, so
it's bingo. The gray emcee,

when he pulls I-18,
cracks the same
joke: "My favorite
words to hear
in the dark? I 18. I 18."
It's dark all right.
The numbers
glib as superlative.
After our tussles, turns out
the dancer liked
to chat. Sweet,
but also, yikes.

Dad's hustle, Mom's ill-
considered likes?
"In today's world," I said,
like an undergrad.
Oh bootlicker, he flickered,
optimistically . . .
            I've been rising,
my own Peter Principle.
Belt and suspenders,
my risk, felt.
And the urban dream
of a bathtub, dishwasher,
and washer/dryer set:
they say you can't

have all three. I can
hear the phrase
"love what you do"—
the new coup,
meaning, of course, the old—
in the invisible store,
hollow idol. I want them all.
Today is Thursday.
I huff essential oils.
Will my downgrade,
a trader, crack his shot

like a sexy golfer, slacks
on the Nasdaq floor?
No more.

I'm swearing off
erotics
as slant facts.
The diminished self.
What's pure
is the gulf
of a slurred
afternoon, near the end
of the week, but not quite.
The blue
on the back of my shoe
obscures
the font
of a luxury word.

And the love has not.

The Turn of the Year

after Donald Justice

I'm not myself.
Refusal
is what suffices—
it has to.
I
widen my horizon,

my horizon
myself,
an imaginary *i*.
Or the bent *f* in *refusal*.
One suffices.
This is what it's come to.

I'm coming to.
On the horizon,
the city suffices.
I like it myself,
the steel refusal
eye

to eye.
To
refusal!
Clouds on the horizon.
My self
is what suffices—

when it suffices.
Aye aye,
I say to myself
(my captain), to
a horizon
the hue of refusal . . .

Like first refusal,
wish suffices.
Goodbye, horizon,
I
murmur to
anybody, which is to say: myself.

from *Complaint in the Garden*

2004

?

is only something on which to hang
your long overcoat; the slender snake asleep
in the grass; the umbrella by the door;

the black swan guarding the pond.
This ? has trouble in mind: do not ask
why the wind broods, why the light is so unclean.

It is summer, the rhetoric of the field,
its yellow grasses, something unanswerable.
The dead armadillo by the roadside, indecent.

Who cares now to recall that frost once encrusted
the field? The question mark— cousin to the 2,
half of a heart—already has begun its underhanded inquiry.

Poem Beginning with a Line by John Ashbery

Jealousy. Whispered weather reports.
The lure of the land so strong it prompts
gossip: we chatter like small birds
at the edge of the ocean gray, foaming.

Now sand under sand hides
the buried world, the one in which our fathers failed,
the palm frond a dangerous truth
they once believed, and touched. Bloodied their hands.

They once believed. And, touched, bloodied their hands;
the palm frond, a dangerous truth;
the buried world, the one in which our fathers failed.
Now sand under sand hides

at the edge of the ocean: gray, foaming
gossip. We chatter like small birds,
the lure of the land so strong it prompts
jealousy. Whispered weather reports.

Song

In the grainy yellow artless light
a warmth is in the air.
And our fair hero— shirtless, thin—
flips his feathered hair

and gives someone the eye. What's next
is obvious enough,
suitably raw but loving, almost,
and almost never rough.

Remember when pornography
was good: the body hair,
the actors barely legal? Flicks
from 1984

past the scary seventies
of bearish men and Crisco,
seeing them fuck to classic rock,
or even worse, to disco—

but still before the mild age
when all the oversexed
were forced to slip a condom on
and get their bottoms waxed.

"There are sites, you know, a few online,"
a friend of mine has said,
"that list the names of porno stars,
the ones who end up dead."

These lines are for the age before
the age of styling gel
and muscle queens, for pretty men
with names like Cal and Joel,

whose sort of lethal innocence
is stirring to the soul,

pale and sweet and having *Fun*
Down in the Glory Hole.

Eros

Giving the man behind the counter my money,
I take from him a fresh white towel
and walk into the sex club—the safe
one—called, mythically, Eros.
I go there, as one does, to kill an hour
or two in the hopeful dark.

Out of my clothes, I step into the dark
of the back rooms, where not money
but flesh is the currency of the hour.
I wrap my torso in the towel
and grab a condom: at Eros,
the only sex allowed is safe,

management insisting that we "Play safe
or be thrown out" into the outer dark.
Life's much simpler inside Eros,
where for a little money
I find what I need, in my towel,
cruising the sticky floors for an hour.

But it's been nearly an hour,
and nothing—I am not going to be safe
with just anyone! Then a man without a towel—
beautiful, in the dark—
puts a hand on my chest. He smells like money.
This is why I go to Eros.

(It's hardly my first Eros
experience: there comes an hour
when, in spite of the money,
no matter how unsafe,
I find what I need only in the dark.)
The man without a towel

removes my towel:
I fall into the arms of Eros;

that world, an underworld, dark
no matter the hour.
And it is good. And we are safe.
It is good to have more sex than money.

Complaint of the Regular

The Lady Pearl attempts to sing along—
Thursday's the designated night of drag.
This queen is ruining my favorite song.

Her dress is cherry-red and overlong,
her entrance undercut—it hit a snag.
The Lady Pearl attempts to sing along:

she sashays sluttishly between the throng
of boys and waves a tiny rainbow flag.
This queen is ruining my favorite song:

you see, "A Foggy Day" does not belong
to her: she's white; her wig is carpet shag
the Lady Pearl attempts to sing along

with Billie Holiday, but all along
her lips are slightly out of sync. This hag,
this queen, is ruining my favorite song.

I come here Thursday nights, and how I long
to look away, but can't. An aging fag—
the Lady Pearl attempts to sing along.
She cannot help but ruin my favorite song.

Complaint of the Lecturer

The classrooms speak in the language of dust—
when the ancient bell rings, the unattainable

fraternity boys rush to the outside fountain
to absolve themselves. I love to watch them.

Design, industry, and practicality have come together:
the height of the shrubs has been calculated;

the eyes of the plumed mascot are like hard zeros.
In the ladies' toilet are bins for used needles.

Look: on the sidewalk, someone has drawn
a chalk outline of a small dead boy, his white blood;

his hair, perverted into a style much too stylish.
I have learned to hate this emptiness,

the emptying of the dumpsters at dusk,
the emptied offices, the emptied bookshelves,

the empty hands of the head librarian.

The Heron

A pond the color of oolong teas.
A heron refusing to look anywhere but east.

Mangroves flecked with a fire,
deep-set birches rife

with the wait for night. In stone,
the heron stares: the stoic tones

of the sky a storied procession of palms;
their red-tipped fronds, overhanging lamps.

Water-bird, it has been centuries since I felt
anything for you. You have been left:

look around. Why does the owl
rest on a goddess's shoulder while you wade so low?

The Revival of Vernacular Architecture

Even the habit of the violet hour,
that measured folding-over into dark,
will not compare to rural dusk right there—
no soot, no one on 301. In Starke

the dirt is fine, is civilized—its worth
is undersold, its rows can only mean
that there the earth's unready for rebirth.
And in between the miles of rain, and rain

between a field, and houses sitting dumb,
I saw a tent, undulant; a cross;
the silhouettes of seated souls; a choir.

I stopped the car, I heard some martyrdom
behind the lamplit tarp. Despite wet grass,
I saw a farmer heal his field with fire.

The Shortened History of Florida

The white men far across the unknown ocean.
The one famous dog, named Becerrillo.
The spotted, wrinkled skin of Ponce de León.
The bones littered in Cayo Hueso.

The horses eaten at Apalachicola Bay.
The gold, like lightning: everywhere, nowhere.
The Cradle and the Grave Company.
The water lilies slowly moving toward the shore.

The scars of cannon fire, the fort's reminder.
The French, half-asleep, half-dressed.
The great Turtle Mound near Coronado.

The long-robed friars and the Indian, Peter.
The Indians, who sometimes killed a priest.
The days of lighthouses, before the Weather Bureau.

The Landscape of Deception

A lone hawk hovers above a corridor
       of gray-boned winter trees
as if it exists only to be admired.
         Early March, the Japanese tulip

in bloom, and the Bradford pear,
       its flowers like boutonnieres—
too white for any boy, any ritual—
       but this is only false spring;

everything here is false, beauty not truth:
       the falling, falling
petals of the Japanese tulip
       already turning ugly,

those petals on the dead grass
       a congregation of deception;
the Bradford pear a lie—
       it will never, to spite its own name,

bear fruit. And the hawk?
       In wait for the small, for the weak,
a lone hawk hovers above a corridor
       of gray-boned winter trees.

Pantoum

If there is a word in the lexicon of love,
it will not declare itself.
The nature of words is to fail
men who fall in love with men.

It will not declare itself,
the perfect word. *Boyfriend* seems ridiculous:
men who fall in love with men
deserve something a bit more formal.

The perfect word? Boyfriend? Ridiculous.
But *partner* is . . . businesslike—
we deserve something a bit less formal,
much more in love with love.

But if partner is businesslike,
then *lover* suggests only sex,
is too much in love with love.
There is life outside of the bedroom,

and lover suggests only sex.
We are left with *roommate,* or *friend.*
There is life, but outside of the bedroom.
My *friend* and I rarely speak of one another.

To my left is my roommate, my friend.
If there is a word in the lexicon of love,
my friend and I rarely speak it of one another.
The nature of words is to fail.

Evidence

Blue is the evidence of what I do,
the lies I'll leave behind, no more, no less.
This is the past, and so it must be true.

This stack of DVDs, of overdue
pornography, the titles meaningless:
blue is the evidence of what I do.

This is the coat from Saks Fifth Avenue,
charged to my old American Express—
this is the past, and so it must be true

that once I loved this wretched shade of blue.
I dreamed of men whom I could not impress.
Blue is the evidence of what I do,

the letter here that ends in *I love you.*
My prose was from the heart, my heart a mess.
This is the past, and so it must be true

I lacked the guts to send it off—I knew
of certain things that one should not confess.
Blue is the evidence of what I do.
This is the past, and so it must be true.

Fiduciary

the relationship between
       blackbird and fence post, between
the cow and its egret, the field
       and wildflowers overrunning the field—
so little depends upon their trust.

       Here, in God we trust
to keep our cash and thoughts in line—
       in the sky, an unexplained white line
could be the first of many omens.
       But this is no country for omens,

the line as chalky as the moon,
       bleak and useless as the moon
now rising like a breath of cold air . . .
       There is gullibility in the air.

The End of the Last Summer

The good white laundry
              dreamlike between white dogwoods;
the Spanish moss; the palm-flanked
              Baptist churches
along the small hill of Eighth Avenue—

none of this matters.
              This landscape is just too much.
The termites are too busy,
              eating the heart
of the wood of the houses of the dead.

—Seven years have passed
              since the red, long-faced tourists
mailed their glossy postcards home,
              regaling friends
with tales of the Gainesville student murders.

All is as it was
              before the murders. The dead?
Names spray-painted on a wall;
              trees providing
shade for the brick, the undergraduates.

It's time to leave now.
              The old professors have gone
on sabbatical, across
              the Atlantic
to visit their favorite fallen empires.

The hidden tree frogs
              have begun to chirp again.
The peninsula grows dark;
              the dead stay dead.
The sea is rising . . . and the world is sand.

from *Breakfast with Thom Gunn*

2009

Early Morning on Market Street

The moon, once full, is snow.
The line of transplanted trees,
thin and bloodless. The pink neon
bakery sign, *Sweet Inspiration,*

a mockery of loneliness—
but no one cares to eat, we souls
of this hour jacked up on what-
ever. And though desire

is a dirty word these days, what
else to call the idling car, its passenger door
pushed open; or the shirtless man—
he must be mad, tweaked out on speed—

outside his door
at Beck's Motor Lodge, staring
for hunger or mercy. Or me,
rubbing dirt from my eyes, wanting,

again, a man I do not want.

Politics

This is what he dreams of:
a map of burned land,
a mound of dirt
in the early century's winter.

A map of burned land?
A country is razed
in the early century's winter.
And God descends.

A country is raised
because of industry.
And God descends,
messengers rush inside

because of industry,
in spite of diplomats.
Messengers rush inside
to haunt the darkened aisles.

In spite of diplomats,
the witnesses know well
to haunt the darkened aisles,
experimentally—

the witnesses know well
that ushers dressed in black
experimentally
lurk by the cushioned seats.

That ushers dress in black
should tell you something:
lurking by the cushioned seats,
the saved and the terrible.

I should tell you something:
this is what he dreams of,

the saved and the terrible—
a mound of dirt.

Queen Christina

To celebrate his final Pride, in June,
my friend, lymphatic, thin, and in distress,
managed to dress in drag. He shot the moon:
outstretched, he'd used his dying to think—obsess—

about the Prada pumps, their skin a snake;
the heavy pantyhose, two pair; the moot
but lacy underthings; the makeup, cake,
to overlay his pain. I called him *beaut-*

i-ful; he said he felt like Greta Garbo
in *Queen Christina* (our campy interplay);
I countered that he looked more like a hobo-
sexual in heels. We howled. That day,

we never left his Castro flat. His rhinestone
glittered, and everywhere, the smell of cologne.

The Mortician in San Francisco

This may sound queer,
but in 1985 I held the delicate hands
of Dan White:
I prepared him for burial; by then, Harvey Milk
was made monument—no, myth—by the years
since he was shot.

I remember when Harvey was shot:
twenty, and I knew I was queer.
Those were the years,
Levi's and leather jackets holding hands
on Castro Street, cheering for Harvey Milk—
elected on the same day as Dan White.

I often wonder about Supervisor White,
who fatally shot
Mayor Moscone and Supervisor Milk,
who was one of us, a Castro queer.
May 21, 1979: a jury hands
down the sentence, seven years—

in truth, five years—
for ex-cop, ex-fireman Dan White,
for the blood on his hands;
when he confessed that he had shot
the mayor and the queer,
a few men in blue cheered. And Harvey Milk?

Why cry over spilled milk,
some wondered, semi-privately, for years—
it meant "one less queer."
The jurors turned to White.
If just the mayor had been shot,
Dan might have had trouble on his hands—

but the twelve who held his life in their hands
maybe didn't mind the death of Harvey Milk;

maybe, the second murder offered him a shot
at serving only a few years.
In the end, he committed suicide, this Dan White.
And he was made presentable by a queer.

Bernal Hill

Something has to give.
We stand above it all.
Below, the buildings' tall
but tiny narrative.

The water's always near,
you say. And so are you,
for now. It has to do.
There's little left to fear.

A wind so cold, one might
forget that winter's gone.
The city lights are on
for us, to us, tonight.

Ruin

Already Judah Street awaits the rain
of streetcar-whine down avenues of rain—
the snap of black umbrellas, the falling coin.
We strangers on the train ignore the rain,
observe two boys in neon slickers run
to catch their bus. Too late! Stuck in the rain,
the boy who's taller smacks the smaller one,
his passion given license by the rain.

I had a birthday yesterday. It's mine:
perversion, self-deceit, nostalgia, rain.
(My stop. I'll brush against a dozen men
before I disembark into the rain
an older, rumpled man. If life is ruin,
then let it burn like Rome, like Dante's rain.)

Last Call

A giant bird-
of-paradise
has climbed the bar:
in this paradise

there are no flowers,
no flowers at all.
When Happy Hour
becomes Last Call—

Adam in drag
our royalty—
we buy her gin
for eternity

(an unseen deejay
scores the years
with pulsing music
of the spheres).

Now the queen has gone,
gone again
in search of love,
in search of sin.

It's closing time.
You were not at fault.
I drain my glass
and lick the salt.

Syntax

Those were the flannel days, after
the Gainesville slayings, before the state
turned permanent red, AIDS still a reason
to cash in your 401(k)—in other words,

the early nineties. Yikes. And I
was a raver in Florida—whistle, bad skin,
snazzy backpack. I learned that the rope
isn't velvet; there never was a rope,

just some feral queen at the door:
Miss Thing, there is no guest list tonight!
Once in, one ate, in designated order,
a few choice letters of the alphabet . . .

I took a choking drag of a clove.
The letters tasted bitter, like love.

The End of Landscape

There's a certain sadness to this body of water
adjacent to the runway, its reeds and weeds,
handful of ducks, the water color

man-made. A still life. And still
life's a cold exercise in looking back,
back to Florida, craning my neck

like a sandhill crane in Alachua Basin.
As for the scrub oaks,
the hot wind in the leaves *was* language,

Spanish moss—dusky, parasitic—
an obsession: I wanted to live in it.
(One professor in exile did,

covered himself in the stuff as a joke—
then spent a week removing mites.) That's
enough. The fields of rushes lay filled

with water, and I said farewell,
my high ship an old, red Volvo DL,
gone to another coast, another peninsula,

one without sleep or amphibious music.
Tonight, in flight from San Francisco—
because everything is truer at a remove—

I watch the man I love watch
the turn of the Sacramento River, then Sacramento,
lit city of legislation and flat land.

I think of Florida, how flat.
I think of forgetting Florida.
And then the landscape grows black.

Breakfast with Thom Gunn

in memory, 1929–2004

We choose a cheap hotel
because they're serving drinks.
We drink. I hear him tell
a tale or two: he thinks

that so-and-so's a sleaze;
and then there was the time
that Miłosz phoned, oh *please*.
Another gin with lime?

I want to say that once,
I saw him dressed in leather,
leaning on a fence
inside a bar. Rather,

walking to the N,
I gush about his books;
he gives his change to men
who've lost their homes and looks:

how like him, I've been told.
Our day together done,
I hug him in the cold.
And then the train is gone.

Ovid in San Francisco

The ancient moon began to rise.
On Market Street, in fierce disguise,
the goddess Fama told me lies

about an older man who turns
to find his lover boy—then learns
the boy's been lost to one who earns

a seven-figure salary,
who owns an urban gallery
and counts his every calorie.

Another accidentally
exposed himself to HIV.
his dust became a cypress tree.

The muscle queen who's wearing red
to coax his husband into bed?
He'll end up getting burned, she said.

I promptly walked away before
she told a tale of guile or gore;
I stepped into Medea's store

in search of anti-aging cream.
Medea hummed *A Love Supreme*—
and in her eyes, a spiteful gleam.

The Long View

Two lovers sit atop
Dolores Park: they stop
their argument to see
a church, a bridge, a sea.

They play a little game:
each man proceeds to name
his list of lovers, dead.
There's no one left unsaid.

Anxious pigeons wait
for crumbs to fall. It's late.
The weather starts to shift:
all fog, all love, will lift.

N

has crawled out of the ocean
to carry us from sleep, like sleep,

the gray of Outer Sunset portending
the gray of Inner Sunset. And so on.

On the N, one should invent
intricate fictions for the lives

of the passengers: time is a game.
Soon we will be underground.

But first, the long lush green
of Duboce Park, the happiness of dogs!

Goodbye now to their owners
eyeing one another. Goodbye

to the park's locked men's room,
where once a man was found dead,

his penis shoved into his own mouth.
The world continues, the engine

of the world the letter N.

Ocean Beach

seems cruel this August,
the skeletal chill,
even the gulls a little
ambivalent. There are

warnings everywhere,
what passes for warning:
kelp like dead sea
creatures, ropy tails and flies;

the dog stalking the crow.
There's no getting around it,
either, the water, its epic
associations, etc.,

the foggy pull of the tide
toward the belated,
the false, the near tears. Beauty lies,
lies in unbeauty.

Translation

In the half-mist of Golden Gate Park,
new friends of friends, barely legal, swig
malt liquor, and I confuse The Shins
with Death Cab for Cutie (the kids snicker,
fiercely; I admire that). Cut grass

smells like sincerity: one Saturday,
long ago, my father, a suburban dream, sweaty
from yard work, took a call (his father, dying).
He sobbed, which unsettled, unsettles, me.
I am neither young nor old.

Lexington

There were horses in the field
on Harrisburg Road; and, further,
the adult theater. (*Look away,* Mother said.) After

the incidents at the sitter's house—
her son Jim; the *Hustler* in the basement;
a red scratch on my neck—

my sister and I were made *latchkey kids.*
And of course I loved the freedom:
crunching sugar cubes until it hurt; *Guiding Light;*

masturbating just out of sight
of my little sister. In the hours after
the indignities of elementary school, before

the return of the parents—that opening—
I started to feel something. It was contempt.

from *Straight Razor*

2013

The Fall of 1992

Gainesville, Florida

An empire of moss,
        dead yellow, and carapace:
that was the season
        of gnats, amyl nitrite, and goddamn
rain; of the gator in the fake lake rolling

his silverish eyes;
        of vice; of *Erotica*,
give it up and let
        me have my way. And the gin-soaked dread
that an acronym was festering inside.

Love was a doorknob
        statement, a breakneck goodbye—
and the walk of shame
        without shame, the hair disheveled, curl
of Kools, and desolate birds like ampersands . . .

I re-did my face
        in the bar bathroom, above
the urinal trough.
        I liked it rough. From behind the stall,
Lady Pearl slurred the words: *Don't hold out for love.*

Straight Razor

He slid the stiff blade up to my ear:
oh, fear,

this should have been thirst, a cheapening act.
But I lacked,

as usual, the crucial disbelief. Sticky, cold,
a billfold

wet in my mouth, wrists bound by his belt,
I felt

like the boy in a briny night pool, he who found
the drowned

body, yet still somehow swam with an unknown joy.
That boy.

Cockroach

You may not remember me.
I lived in Sand Lake Hills,
where there was sand, but no lake,
no hills; I lived in half-truths.

I was gated. I played
with my Anne Sexton
action figures; I played adolescence.
Nothing came between me

and my Calvins, not really,
and I was gay for pay—
not really. I was the kid in Fairvilla Video
with a taste for gang bangs.

Is it all coming back to you now,
like a chalkboard song?
I was the canvasser in front of Walgreens,
the one you almost never avoided.

I was Mr. Roboto, thank you
very much: I was another punch card
at the computer center. I was code,
a cloud of Drakkar Noir

in the Shady Oaks mall
men's room. I was a hangnail,
the garnish in your cocktail.
I was your cockroach in Orlando,

the one who crawled on you at night.

My Guidance Counselor

He smelled of smoke and Velamints,
his purple tie like violence.

He told me, "Son, this questionnaire
indicates you like good hair,

Satyricon, and Panda Express.
Uh-huh. Perhaps we should address

your stares at Coach Mancini's shorts.
He's filed a few detailed reports.

It isn't pretty. Nor are you,
your spotty face and Dippity-do.

Avert your eyes. Buy some tail
on lurid Orange Blossom Trail.

You and I are one disease.
We both look well enough, but please."

Stable

Bloody, slick, and fierce,
I slid out of the womb.
My heart was underfed.
My mouth began to foam.

At six I bit my lip
and took to backyard voguing:
I struck a rigid pose
in vigilante leggings.

I stole our family hearse.
I had the goods to sell.
My underpants were used:
he liked that they were small.

At twenty-one I bought
a microwave and warmed
a frozen Hungry Man.
My bachelorhood, confirmed.

(For *six* read *seventeen,*
for *microwave* read *purse,*
for *Hungry* read *Alone,*
for *hearse* and *womb* read *horse.*)

I have a private stable.
I roll around and whinny.
I'm dying to be groomed.
So here's your pile of money,

and there's my pile of oats.
I'll let you brush my mane.
Just promise me you'll keep
your mouth away from mine.

End Words

in memory of Reetika Vazirani (1962–2003)
and Rachel Wetzsteon (1967–2009)

Sewanee, Tennessee.
Summer of '96, I went there for
booze and poetry and rest.
I danced a little dance;
I talked a little shop.
I forgot a recent ghost.

"Invitation to a Ghost"
was my favorite poem in Tennessee.
And Justice taught my workshop.
(God love him, he called me decadent for
ending a line with an anapest.) At the dance
party with Allison and the rest

of the poets from Rebel's Rest,
ambition was the ghost
unseen, but always in attendance.
And I misplaced my faith in Tennessee,
upon a hill: I gave an undergrad what for
after priming him with lines of Bishop.

Gossip is another word for *talking shop.*
But Rachel, sharper than the rest,
winner of things I hoped for,
was above all that, like a charming host.
She spoke of posterity in Tennessee.
And every day felt like a dance

preparing us for a bigger dance.
In the bookstore, I pretended to shop
with Reetika, Rachel's roommate in Tennessee,
wicked-funny and stunning and rest-
less. We flirted like we stood a ghost
of a chance. I was twenty-four.

I wonder now what it's all been for:
that summer; the words; the awful dance
that followed. So many ghosts.
Let the muses close the horror shop.
Let Rachel and Reetika rest.
—Years ago, there was Tennessee.

September Elegies

in memory of Seth Walsh, Justin Aaberg, Billy Lucas,
and Tyler Clementi

There are those who suffer in plain sight,
there are those who suffer in private.
Nothing but secondhand details:
a last shower, a request for a pen, a tall red oak.

There are those who suffer in private.
The one in Tehachapi, aged 13.
A last shower, a request for a pen, a tall red oak:
he had had enough torment, so he hanged himself.

The one in Tehachapi, aged 13;
the one in Cooks Head, aged 15:
he had had enough torment, so he hanged himself.
He was found by his mother.

The one in Cooks Head, aged 15.
The one in Greensburg, aged 15:
he was found by his mother.
"I love my horses, my club lambs. They are the world to me,"

the one in Greensburg, aged 15,
posted on his profile.
"I love my horses, my club lambs. They are the world to me."
The words turn and turn on themselves.

Posted on his profile,
"Jumping off the gw bridge sorry":
the words turn, and turn on themselves,
like the one in New Brunswick, aged 18.

Jumping off the gw bridge sorry.
There are those who suffer in plain sight
like the one in New Brunswick, aged 18.
Nothing but secondhand details.

Song

I found my muster station, sir.
My skin is patent leather.
The tourists are recidivists.
This calm is earthquake weather.

I've used up all the mulligans.
I'd kill to share a vice.
The youngster reads a yellowed *Oui.*
The socialite has lice.

The Europe trip I finally took
was rash and Polaroid,
was gilt, confit, and bathhouse foam.
And I cannot avoid

the end: I will not die in Paris,
won't rest for good behind
a painted mausoleum door.
The purser will not find

me mummified beneath your tulle,
and Paris will not burn.
Today is Thursday, so I'll die.
Come help me pick my urn.

Larkin Street

Her shade surprised me,
          the leather lark in the Night Train
dark of Polk Gulch, her arch face
          like a thirty-
day clock on its last ticktock.

I should talk. To think
          I got faux-hawked for this, and waxed
my, um—my strip of anger,
          for a fresh bent.
For, maybe, militainment.

There goes the parade
          of turkey boas and blowback,
of Aqua Net and tight cuts.
          And hanky code:
gray means I'm fit to be tied.

Where does it all end?
          Your shorts. I duck in a dirty
bookstore for sport, look for friends
          on smut boxes;
for one neon word, *Arcade,*

such fun. For a fee.
          When we're through, I'm carving a nick
in your snail trail. That's the poem.
          (I am so sick
of pretending to be me.)

Only You

As I skipped out this morning,
skipping down Castro Street,
the queens upon the asphalt
were racks of hanging meat.

The Pendulum was open.
The Mix had yet to close.
I stepped into the latter
to down a bitter dose.

We danced to "Only You"
by Teddy Pendergrass.
I sniffed a fetid boy.
I felt his denim ass.

The bears admired their beers.
The chat turned flat and racy.
The bartender's a clown—
we call him John Wayne Gacy.

He makes me laugh for breakfast;
he serves me guilt for lunch.
And when it's time for dinner,
he gives my face a punch:

I feign dismay then ask
if I may have another.
He smiles and always says,
I am not your mother.

A bear began to sing:
"The night is falling soon.
And love is never love
without a tub of ruin.

And lounging in the ruin,
what becomes of us?

Narcissus in the water
strangled Commodus."

He sucked a little straw
then shut his fuzzy trap.
This place is just a blemish
on the oblivion map.

I live a block away.
Oh yes, I live alone.
I won't be coming back.
I do not have a phone.

I can't provide the moon.
I hope you've said your prayers.
I have a special room
down the cellar stairs.

Teaser

"Making love" is the most
disconcerting phrase—
just deflect those scare quotes
with the butter knife.

Just look at the sunset, like a tryst
with a realtor—the downturn says,
Now's a good time to hurt.
So where's my Mr. Ward in *Hustler White*,

my dead piece in sheer pants,
floating in an L.A. jacuzzi?
If this were the eighties,
they would throw an Uzi in.

If this were the seventies,
"Two-Fisted Love" by Phoebe Snow.
Are you for sale? You know
you're my boyfriend now. This is the life,

the floating Cuervo bottle like
credibility, classic staging;
this has been a dream of mine:
a handful of your shaved nuts,

which shows a sense of danger;
dry-heave evenings;
and a nod to Kenneth Anger.
We will always live in this jacuzzi.

We will order up a better
version of you, to tease
out metaphors and the night's
mincing poet-voice.

Look at us—we're smarter
than our hair! No choice.

Now let me stick this little strip
of duct tape on your lips.

Gossip, like mercy, gets us nowhere.

Hyperbole

I start with good intentions. On a date,
I struggle not to sound so insincere;
I think, hyperbole will be my fate.

Last night I found a fairly decent mate.
When cruising for a partner on the pier,
I start with good intentions, on a date.

Last night was filled with ways to fabricate
affection: tulips; lube; imported beer,
I think. Hyperbole will be my fate:

I left before he might reciprocate;
I swallowed so his mother wouldn't hear.
I start with good intentions on a date—

my upswept hair; my briefs. I'm losing weight.
What stays, like some insipid trick, is fear.

But Enough about Me

The light is getting nearer.
I hope to find a lover.
I grab a hand mirror
and fluff my comb-over.

My shoes will hide the warts;
my hand, my grubby mouth.
My khakis smother farts,
allusion muffles truth.

My formalism blinds
the critics. Like a star.
(My bio note reminds
the groupies not to stare.)

I need to sneak a smoke
before I hit the gym,
before I stroke a bloke.
I like them lean and dumb.

I like that turning forty
wasn't such a biggie.
I bought myself a party:
his name was Little Piggy.

I'll win the Prix de Rome.
I'll travel on the trains.
I'll write my poem of Rome,
"A Randy Life in Ruins."

But this is not a train.
A train is what I pull.
You drink to kill pain;
I'm pushing in your stool.

The Lion's Mouth

I walk into a stanza.
There's decent gin here;
the men are critically tanned
in winter. The gin kicks in;

our eyes get all misty from an indrawn
loss, eyes bright and dead as stars
on someone's Walk of Fame.
I walk in. I walk.
I raise my highball, to no one.

Which is to say, to you.
My bow tie misses your bow tie.
My cords miss yours. Who says
that love isn't sartorial?
Every pull of an argyle, every loop
reminds me, a little bit, of you.
This is embarrassing; this is also true.

Night comes, its one-sidedness.
I think I'll call in sick.
I think I'll go to I don't know,
to Venice, to feel something.
It's good for that.

I go to Venice. No, not that one.

I go all the way to Venice.
I get the Ezra Pound haircut,
have a leering coffee break.
Mostly I go for the goodbye, the first,
cheerless stretch on the Eurostar,
because leaving it,
I tell myself, is more freighted
than leaving you. Just look. I left you
six years ago and still can't believe.

Goodbye Venice; goodbye dogfight
and glut. I left you. I left so many
anonymous denunciations in the lion's mouth.

Untoward Occurrence at Embassy Suites Poetry Reading

after Marilyn Hacker

First I want to thank you all for coming,
for standing so patiently in line.
I know these are difficult times.
I know some of us hold the system in contempt.
So it's a helluva time for poetry to be in fashion.
Most readings, I aim to undermine things with pronoun

slippages and rot. I'm very pro-noun.
I often sing about the joy of coming,
how much I secretly love adverbs and fashion,
and walking pensively at dusk on the High Line,
filled with just the right amount of contempt
for my own deceit. Good times.

But this is not one of those times.
Tonight, I'd like to talk about one pronoun:
you. And one noun: contempt.
I have seen you coming
and going at this conference, debuting your line,
checking your font in the mirror. Fashion

is important to people who write in fashion.
I'm not saying I don't. the times are the times.
But I have watched you nod at a terrible line.
I have watched you sit stone-faced at pronoun
confusion, and, though you saw it coming
a mile away, smile at a dull allusion to *Contempt*.

Tonight I reserve my contempt
for you, audience. Per the fashion,
a few insurgents are coming
to take care of you. Sign of the times.
Trust me, I'm a pro. Noun?
Verb? Object? Casualties of the line.

Now you're near the end. I cut the line.
The gas is seeping in the vents, like contempt.
The blood is as slick as a pronoun.
Your bodies will be arranged in the latest fashion.
Your friends will read about you in the *Times*.
The doors are bolted. You can't stop what's coming.

American Apparel

This glaring, unfathomable
San Francisco summer fog is
like eternity, like plain speech.

One cannot resect the unresectable.
What I mean is, one cannot
remove all ornament or longing—

the previous stanza, for instance, was lit
like seventies porn. Sure, we get our nut
behind the green door,

but the list of details—
the *tall drink of water,* the *oh god yes*—
eventually glug-glugs out by the watercooler.

Is this one more elaborate joke? This
is another push-poll, right? Yeah,
right. The republic is whimpering—

like what? Like, nothing. The stats
have been summarized, the Scantrons
filled in. How astonishingly green. How fitting.

from *Proprietary*

2017

Proprietary

In a precisely lighted room, the CFO speaks
of start-to-start dependencies.
Says let me loop back with you.

Says please cascade as appropriate.
It's that time of morning; we all can smell
the doughnut factory. If scent were white

noise, doughnuts would be that scent.
The factory won't sell at any price.
The building next to it burns the animals

we experiment on. I have worked
on a few preclinical reports in my time.
The rhesus monkeys become

so desperate that they attempt suicide,
over and over again. I am legally obligated
to spare you the particulars.

How could things be any different?
Here many choice molecules have been born.
Here. This pill will dissolve like sugar.

Your last five months will be good ones.

Nothing

My mother is scared of the world.
She left my father after forty years.
She was like, Happy anniversary, goodbye;

I respect that.
The moon tonight is dazzling, is full
of itself if not quite full.

A man should not love the moon, said Miłosz.
Not exactly. He translated himself
as saying it. A man should not love translation;

there's so much I can't know. An hour ago,
marking time with someone I would like to like,
we passed some trees and there were crickets

(crickets!) chirping right off Divisadero.
I touched his hand, and for a cold moment
I was like a child again,

nothing more, nothing less.

Black Box

I was someone's
honor student once,
a sticker, a star.
I aced Home Ec and Geometry;

I learned to stab a fork,
steer my mother's car.
Old enough to work,
I refreshed the salad bar

at Steak and Ale,
scarcity a line
I couldn't fail.
The summers between university,

I interned at AT&T,
in the minority
outreach they called *Inroads*.
My boss, Vicki, had two

roommates, whom she
called, simply, The Gays,
crashing on her floor.
That was before

I was gay, I won't try to say
with a straight face.
Like anyone really cares
I care. What I'm trying to say:

all this prepared
me for these squat blinking
office accessories.
The dry drinking

after the accidental reply-all.
By now there's a lot to lose.

Little by little, I have become
so careful, no talk

of politics or orientation:
I let them say, He's a *homosexual,*
without an arch correction.
At a fondue buffet

in Zurich, our dumb-
founded senior group
director—when I let slip,
damn it, my trip

with a twenty-year-old—inquired,
They're always over seventeen,
right? I told her of course,
god yes, and, seething, smiled,

which I'm famous for.
I didn't want to scare
her. But I tell you,
I'm keeping score.

E-mail is no more
than a suicide
I'd like to please recall.
Note my suicide.

I'm paid to multitask,
scramble the life
out of fun:
Monday I will ask you—

every dash a loaded gun,
every comma, a knife—
to bury the black-box file.

Order

For once, he was just my father.
We drove to the Computing Center
in a Monte Carlo Landau
not technically ours. Lexington,

1977. That fall. The color
had settled, too, undone
orange-brown and dull yellow,
crimson. And it was something,

yet not, the pile of leaves
just a pile of leaves. Sorry to think
what thinking has done to landscape:
he loved punched cards,

program decks and subroutines,
assembly languages
and keypunch machines.
Even my father looked small

next to a mainframe.
The sound of order;
the space between us.
We almost laughed, but not for years—

we almost laughed. But not. For years,
the space between us,
the sound of order
next to a mainframe.

Even my father looked small.
And keypunch machines,
assembly languages,
program decks and subroutines.

He loved punched cards,
what thinking has done to landscape—

just a pile of leaves. Sorry to think,
yet not, the pile of leaves

crimson. And it was. Something
orange-brown and dull yellow
had settled, too, undone
1977, that fall, the color

not technically ours, Lexington
in a Monte Carlo Landau.
We drove to the Computing Center.
For once he was just, my father.

Florida

Like eelgrass through a glass-
bottom boat on the Silver River,
I see the state, obscured yet pure. Derision,

a tattooed flame crackling
underneath the lewd, uncool
khaki of an amused park worker.

I was the sometimes boy on a leash,
my sliver of assent in 1984—
as if it were my decision.

The I-75 signage, more than metaphor.
As if I had the right to vote.
The slumber parties then were hidden wood;

the tea so sweet, the saccharin
pink and artificial, like intelligence.
The science sponsored in part by chance.

I made my acting debut with the red
dilettante down the street, "Rusty" Counts,
in *Rusty Counts Presents: Suburbs of the Dead,*

straight to VHS. My parents phoned a counselor.
A palmetto bug read *Megatrends* on the fold-
ing chair by our aboveground swimming pool . . .

The pool shark lurked, but not to fear.
The end unknowable, blue, inmost, and cold,
like the consolation of a diplomatic war.

Proximity

Out of the fog comes a little white bus.
It ferries us south to the technical mouth
of the bay. This is biopharma, Double Helix Way.

In the gleaming canteen, mugs have been
dutifully stacked for our dismantling,
a form of punishment.

Executives take the same elevator as I.
This one's chatty, that one's gravely engrossed
in his cloud. Proximity measures shame.

I manage in an office, but an office
that faces a hallway, not the bay. One day
I hope to see the bay that way. It all began

in the open, a cubicle—there's movement.
My door is always open, even when I shut it.
I sit seven boxes below the CEO

on the org chart. It's an art, the *value-add,*
the compound noun. *Calendar* is a verb.
To your point, the kindest prepositional phrase.

Leafy trees grow a short walk from Building 5.
Take a walk. It might be nice to lie and watch the smoky
marrow rise and fall, and rise. Don't shut your eyes.

Realtor

Please
consider Ocean Beach
out of reach.
Try not to gulp
the green water
we porpoise
like employees.
My purpose:
your thought-partner.

There is a feeling
just shy of feeling,
like tongue on teeth.
Disbelief
hangs there,
an ill-chosen comma,
a lanyard with a pass.
I swear the train is coming.
I'm only here to help.

A client bought,
on second thought,
that *House in Vermont.*
Night is flirty words
with fiends,
the phlebotomists
from Quest
boning up on Thoreau.
It's too soon to throw

in the cards.
Live and let give?
Here. Let me give
you the *high five.*
I searched;

my activism,
lightly starched.
I never meant
to live in euphemism.

Halston

Roy Halston Frowick, 1932–1990

He kept his middle name, the pick of the lot,
he thought, and mispronounced himself: *Hall-stun.*

At Bergdorf's he acquired an accent and referred
to himself in the third person, every bird he flayed

wrapped in Ultrasuede. He lit a True with a True,
smeared his hirsute muse with sequins. There were air-

kisses, Capote's new-cut face at Studio 54, that Baccarat
flute of ejaculate. Never too late, he ordered in

meat and potatoes, and a trick.
He called it "dial-a-steak, dial-a-dick." He appeared

on *The Love Boat,* Halstonettes in tow,
maybe the high, maybe the low, watermark.

When his pupils betrayed him at work, on came the shades.
And a well-cut blazer, paranoia. He had signed away

the rights to his name, for options. When he tried
to reclaim them from the conglomerate,

he excused himself to the toilet, just a sec—
white dust on a black turtleneck.

His block started to look a lot like sickness.
Even his beloved orchids, the sickness.

Just like that, the eighties were gone.
New York, New York, the eighties were no one.

Leo & Lance

for David Trinidad

I was seventeen
in Orlando,
heading toward

Orange Blossom Trail,
where the porn was.
Fairvilla Video,

its fried, freshened air.
I was terrified
but also thrilled,

on the edge.
Can anyone even
remember how hard-

won a little corner
of sex was then,
no Internet,

no hope,
no combination?
I can't; I can.

In an
elaborate bid
to convince

myself and the clerk
I was bisexual,
I bought a bisexual

video
that I can't recall,
and a box

that made my heart stop:
Leo & Lance.
(VHS wasn't cheap:

I spent all
my allowance.)
I can measure

this adventure
in increments
of shame:

tape loop,
checkout,
the run-walk

to my red Buick
(no one could miss me),
the peel out.

And the drive home,
anticipation,
cruel cellophane . . .

Leo Ford,
born Leo John Hilgeford,
looked like California

by way of Dayton.
There was his tender
love of Divine,

that rumored three-way
on Fire Island
with Calvin Klein.

Late in his career
he raised rare birds,
volunteered

at Project Angel Food.
He was versatile:
so much to give.

And Lance,
David Alan Reis,
from Santa Barbara,

or maybe Oklahoma.
Poor orphan,
the stints

in jail,
IV drugs,
and conversion.

Leo and Lance
had the chance
to work together

twice on film—
Leo & Lance and
Blonds Do It Best—

and more than once
on the corner.
(Where have all

the hustlers gone,
anyway?)
They died

weeks apart,
in 1991.
Lance first,

in May,
in San Jose,
of AIDS complications.

On the death certificate,
his job is listed
as "model of clothing."

That July,
Leo on his motorcycle
was struck by a truck

on Sunset. "Chillingly,
Leo had played
a motorcycle accident

victim in *Games*,"
says IMDb,
so those who knew

his oeuvre
might have seen it coming.
After the wake at Josie's,

his ashes were scattered
by the Golden Gate Bridge.
A tree in India—

IMDb again,
as if the truth matters—
was planted in his name . . .

As I try
to get this right,
I pull up my cache

of scanned porn.
Leo & Lance:
it begins in synth,

Cali melancholy
canyon light,
and here's Leo,

shirtless,
running up a hill
in tight denim,

letterman jacket
thrown over his shoulder—
now the tinkling

piano; now's a good time
to jerk off
by the last of the snow.

God, bottle-blond Leo.
But wait, who
is that loping up the hill,

gawky, rugged, also blond,
a dumbfounded *wow*
uttered as he watches

Leo shoot? Of course:
it's Lance. Before
they formally meet,

before they go
back to the lodge
and do what they do

better than life,
they have a little snowball fight,
brief, unexpectedly sweet—

like children in the street.

Perspective

Associations
are seductive and global.

Such gestures
seem almost primal,

though it's nothing of the sort.
One can waste

an hour one-upping
Anonymous

in a text,
the right equivocation

and torso pic.
I lost 2010

trying to rhyme *sext*
with *sucked,* or *sacked,*

or, that's it, *sect:*
it's San Francisco,

for the love of Pete.
The meat

lolls on its silver plate.
On Market Street,

a pool of vomit,
a pigeon's meal.

I would eat,
but who eats.

My friend on meth
strapped his infant

to her car seat
one night all night

in the Tenderloin. All
we want

to feel is a full
roll of quarters,

not to feel.
We are art-house stars

in every back room
and alley and stairs . . .

I have options:
undercut what I say

as soon as I say it,
or look you dead

in the face,
a parody of sincerity.

In the front room,
you should be fixing us

a drink, innocuous,
or spreading paste—

perspective—
while in the bedroom, listen,

things only a comedown twink
might dare condone

are proposed to my outcall.
I do. I believe we're done.

Complaint

It was a lower–
       Nob Hill affair, no shower,
no grower, our arc
       like an involuntary spit
at the urinal: a pull; a splash of blue.

How could one predict
       cozy slurs over Sidecars,
strenuous humming?
       Parliament of scowls at the Owl Bar?
But what I would have given. To be a lone,

rolled, superfluous
       r in his world! Compliant,
I measure attempts
       at love against some fictive monster
alive. I lick a fleck of sleep from his eye . . .

The moon is a stye.
       The foyer, my brightest star.
Help me down the line
       of antibacterial goodbye.
The little black car on the screen is coming.

Dolores Park

The palms
are psalms.

The nail salons,
manicured lawns.

This is some phase.
The park has been razed.

I miss the hip,
hours at a clip,

their dopey glazed
Dolores haze

(sorry).
I worry

about basic stuff:
my graying scruff,

Ambien addiction.
Eviction . . .

—But there's another story:
this lawn was once a cemetery.

In 1888,
the late

were stirred,
disinterred,

carted somewhere calm, a
nothing place called Colma.

By then the dead
prohibited

in city light.
They thought this was all right:

the dead have nothing to lose;
the dead were Jews.

Hills of Eternity, Home of Peace:
The dead were put in their place.

Alphabet Street

Prince Rogers Nelson, 1958–2016

"Adore" was my song
Back in '87—
Cool beans, I liked to say,
Desperately uncool.
Except for you.
Florida, a dirty hand
Gesture; the state, pay dirt.
Headphones on, I heard,
In a word, you were sex,
Just in time. Who was I
Kidding? Then, as now,
Love is too weak to define.
Mostly I just ran,
Not yet sixteen,
Overreaching. Track star,
Pretty uniform.
Queer, of course. *Adore.*
Rewind: my beloved teammates
Sometimes called me Cinnamon
Toast Crunch, or CTC, being neither Black nor white.
Until the end of time.
Vanity would never do it for me.
Would you? You were definite, the
X in my fix. And now,
You're gone. The old, on repeat. The new
Zeal: zero.

Translation

So much has gone to shit. My hair. The state.
The addicts lie on Ellis Street, unfathered.
Reporters scribble synonyms for hate:
the men in blue have billy-clubbed the gathered.

And then, as grisly as an accident,
comes love, what feels like love. Befalls
the best of us, as if the discontent
of days were not enough. I make the calls,

or so I think: Desire, that heretic,
is stealing, spider-fingered, all the hours.
The years. My scorn, acutely politic:
I peck him on the cheek, then hit the showers.

—Soapy, erect, I'll conjure up a time
when love was just a fecal, furtive crime.

Young Republican

September 1984.
The heat was like a ray gun.
The Communists had much to fear:
his name was Ronald Reagan—

and so was mine in middle school,
throughout the mock debate.
The recreation hall was full
of democratic hate.

I ended all my thoughts with *well,*
declared my love for Nancy.
My stifling suit was poly-wool.
I sounded like a pansy.

But teachers didn't seem to care
that Ronald Reagan looked
a little fey, and had some flair.
I wanted to be liked,

the boy who mowed the neighbors' yards,
the new kid in Ocala—
while Mondale read his index cards,
I sipped a Coca-Cola

that I had spiked with Mother's gin,
and frowned, and shook my head.
Oh Walter, there you go again,
I smiled and vainly said.

I reenacted getting shot.
I threw benign grenades.
I covered up what I forgot.
I never mentioned AIDS.

Almost

One last meal, family style—
        no family, and with suspect style.
November first, my almost-groom
        fresh off his flasher costume
discharge at the office. Harris tweed.
        I read it on his antisocial feed.

The motel life is all a dream—
        we were, as they say, living the dream.
I appreciate our quandary,
        hot-plate dates and frowsy laundry.
Face tattoos are never a good sign.
        I hope his tumor is benign.

I won't forget the time he lent
        me *Inches,* which I gave up for Lent.
Our love was threat, like phantom pain.
        An almost-plan for a bullet train.
I'm weaning myself off graphic tees,
        not taking on any new disease.

I walk along Pier 5 to kill the myth,
        of course another stab at myth.
I pull my output from the shelf
        and wildly anthologize myself.
I've adopted another yellow lab.
        I hope to die inside this cab.

My lack of faith is punctuation—
        no wait, the lack of punctuation.
Every intonation, one more pact
        with injury; my latest one-act:
Flossing in Public.
        In the spattered glass of the republic.

from *A Better Life*

2021

A Better Life

after Julio Cortázar

It's silly to think
fourteen years ago
I turned thirty.

How I made it that far
I'll never know.
In this city of hills,

if there was a hill
I was over it. Then.
(In queer years,

years
are more than.)
Soon it will be fifteen

since the day I turned thirty.
It's so remote.
I didn't think I'd make it

to fourteen years ago.
Fear lives in the chest
like results.

You say my gray, it makes
me look *extinguished;*
you make me cringe.

I haven't cracked
the spines of certain paperbacks,
or learned a sense of direction,

even with a slick device.
But the spleen doesn't ask twice,
and soon it will be fifteen years

since I turned thirty.
Which may not sound like a lot.
Which sounds like the hinge

of a better life:
It is, and it is not.

Florida Again

I forgave myself for having had a youth.

Thom Gunn

At the Fashion
Square mall,
back
of Waldenbooks,

I see my younger self
haunting
the magazine rack.
Ripping out pages

of *Blueboy,*
tucking them
in a Trapper
Keeper.

Turn back.
His eyes meet mine,
animal
and brittle,

a form
of gratitude
that a man
kept his stare.

Any man.
I half-smile
some admission,
and though

he cannot
see it coming,
I excuse him
his acid jeans;

two Swatch
watches,
two guards.
He, I,

must be
nineteen:
sex was "safer"
then—

scribbles
on the mall
men's room stall;
malaise

of saxophone
and PSAs.
How
did I

even
learn how to live
in 1991?
Landlocked,

cockblocked,
Spanish moss
festering.
I forgive him.

True Blue

The whine
of the 24-
line—
anymore,
what's
it for?
Like a sale
on sale,
I bought
the thought:
I'm not
staying.

Was I
trying
to fit
California
into
Connecticut?
Without
a doubt.
The body
settles
itself—
I lie

on the right
side
of the bed
instead
of hope.
I pick out
and lay out
my workout
outfit
the night

before.
To cope.

Lotions
and potions
lance
emotions.
And a boil.
Silence
your new
humiliation,
a stylistic
tic.
No pic,
no dial.

We'll
always
have Russian
dressing
at the mall,
TGI Fridays.
My oligarch
after dark.
Our plans
second-
hand
fashion.

Middle-
class as
a buffet,
my gay
life measured
out
in Madonna
LPs—please
play
True Blue.

Admit it.
You hate it.

Does that
hurt.
It's not
a question.
Your face
transformed
into a bird's.
You changed
your thoughts
and had
the haunts
of birds.

I scour
the street
for meat.
Controlled
transparency,
the hours.
Flies,
sated
elsewise.
My pump-
and-dump
romance:

goodbye.
You once
said
your safe
word
was *sneeze
guard*—
that's two.
That's us.
Please.

You
are gorgeous.

Rhapsody

1

Pollen.
Fallen
on
men
like soot,
snow,
ash,
cash.
Avoidance
of eye
contact
I
redact
any chance
in advance.

2

Mottled
sheets;
bottled
dets.
Since
when
is urban
hiking?
Get off
my
intellectual
property.
The fog
a feral
dog.

3

Recession:
hairline,
gumline.
Bread-
line.
Passive
regression.
He playcd
the pup;
he played
tricks.
Politics
the infamous
stray
under the bed.

4

Night,
a sex
site
of white
boys
with an
aversion
to latex.
Or, a version
of that.
I bet
not one
of them
has ever
shat.

5

We pause
to disarticulate
our jaws.
Living
Dead
giving
head.
Backdoor
Chip,
my step-
hipster,
my go-
go:
find her
on Grindr.

6

Numbers
in love,
affairs
with shares:
Big Pharma.
Our age
a gag,
a mouthful
of knowledge.
Fierce.
Karma
is workin'
a Birkin
colostomy
bag.

7

He held
an associate's
degree
in manipulation.
His existence,
consonants;
the vowels
like bowels,
no movement.
Beat off,
he yelled;
I think
he meant
buzz.
I did. Both.

8

I resist
the urge
to rhapsodize:
boys
in blue
pills;
the poor;
the purge.
Honor
kills.
At least
his
"grooming
injury"
was "minor."

9

It was:
the butt-
dial
of relationships;
two ships;
philosophy
and pot
brownies
with townies;
a half-
mile
from
thought.
It was
not.

10

I do
as I
am told.
When
he blinks
I call;
when
he smiles
I fold.
I do
it on
a dime.
What's
a dime?
Old.

11

Nail
and doughnut
and dildo
shops:
a full
life.
Become
the dead.
And yet,
sunset:
pre-cum
spread
with
a dull
knife.

RSVP

The scribbled Bible verse in lieu of tip;
the table talk that grins and lays the blame;
the rubber on the bed, its little rip.
The numbers in your phone without a name.

Stalking Points

The coldest
August
in memory:
a lack of trust.

The lumber
of a streetcar
neither
here nor there,

near nor far.
The bros
in boas
are turning back

to Burning Man.
Sidewalks
slumber.
Take a number;

allege
your size.
On my commute,
I saw you

edge
a stranger raw,
then sanitize
those hands

the minute
you got off
the F line.
Awe.

The rage:
engage
in character fights;
dim the pain

like all the lights.
Who doesn't want
to be walked,
by a brute

in a suit,
out of the high-rise?
Who doesn't want
to be stalked.

Everybody Everybody

after Black Box

I do not need a man,
I need a man

with the right
kind of damage. Right.

The word *looking*
means we are looking

dutifully into smart
phones: don't we look smart

in our fleece vests.
Each day an option vests,

our sentence
a declarative sentence:

This is the place.
We know our place.

I trade
tirade

for nothing,
but nothing

is accidental,
or accidental

as collapse.
Remember the collapse?

Nothing exists before
the day before:

I was let go,
and by let go

I mean garden
leave. No garden,

just this little
patch of city, a little

dog shit,
I mean human shit.

And all my ex-
mausoleums on Valencia, ex-

humed as furniture stores;
pastry stores

with animal names.
Or too coy for names.

Come
on! Does it all come

out in the wash?
The great Martha Wash

is on the radio
as if there were radio,

singing her large heart out,
warned never to come out

from behind the screen.
In front of the screen,

a nineties supermodel like a city
lip-syncs—like this city,

emaciated—for everybody.
Everybody.

The Lone Palm

for Kevin Killian, 1952–2019

The chatter,
a little
matter.
The bas-relief,
shallow grief.
Décor,
1930s, or
is it 1980s:

neon signs;
a deco dish
of golden fish;
real fronds
and bottle
blondes
lit
by George Platt Lynes . . .

My friend Kevin
tells a story.
It was 1982;
he stepped into
the Lone Palm.
A bartender,
tall and all
alone,

eager
to be of service:
a nervous
nod,
some code,
meager
speech—
doors locked,

the bar
a makeshift
bed—
it was efficient,
half an hour
at most,
and almost
tender.

Time for the shift.
"What're you doing
next Saturday?
Come by then . . ."
A week passed;
Kevin returned.
"Where's so-and-so,"
he asked,

starting
a description.
"He took a turn
last week and died,"
said the latest
bartender, slow
to answer.
"The gay cancer."

Sometimes,
that's how
it worked—
before
the test.
I'm out of luck,
thought Kevin.
We all were . . .

—It's sentimental,
some say,
to allude

to the plague.
The indignities
of the eighties
and nineties,
an urn

on the mantel.
Keep it vague
because
it's over.
It's never
over.
If it were,
we would all

be at the Lone Palm,
white
tablecloths,
chrome shaker
and a flask:
no need to ask.
Mark has his vision,
James scoffs

at the new
religion,
unmarred
by a purple
lesion—
and right
after Last Call,
we stumble/fall

to 22nd and Guerrero,
kiss each other
on the corner:
fading together,
no one scared.
The night

simplified.
Good night.

Good night.

Weather

The negative of dazzling
                    Donald Britton

I called
in sick
from
my rent-
controlled
den.
Yet
here

I come.
On BART,
I heart
the scent,
a soapy
gent
in my
compartment.

Nice start.
Where
are we?
Look!
The Salesforce
Tower
above
the fog.

It's not
so bad—
a thought.
(To hate
or congratulate
myself?)

Vertical
integration,

a layer.
The Wi-Fi
stable;
at least
the new-
ish
MOMA
tweets

Magritte—
He's decent;
the docent,
triggering.
Pipes
and clouds,
like sketchy
sex.

This
table-book
in the foyer,
bloated
spine!
Who takes
Amex?
Not

mine.
The sun
could be
a doubloon.
The clock
stuck,
belatedly,
at noon.

Anecdote of an Ex-

Cape Town, November 2015

"You should stay in today.
I need to have sex with a stranger.
You can watch, but you can't
join us. Look at that thing on your face.

I need to have sex. With a stranger
who's long enough to hit my spot.
Join us? Look at that thing on your face:
your skin is terrible, those acne scars.

Who's long enough to hit my spot?
Not you. I'm just being honest.
Your skin is terrible, those acne scars—
I keep asking my sister, is Randy even attractive?

Not you. I'm just being honest.
And I have a perfect dick.
I keep asking my sister, is Randy even attractive?
I've been with 800 men; I know what's good,

and I have a perfect dick.
You should really use an enema for once.
I've been with 800 men; I know what's good.
I'd rather watch a two-minute clip.

You should really use an enema. For once,
it might be nice to avoid your shit.
I'd rather watch a two-minute clip:
amateur creampie. Internal breeding.

It might be nice to avoid your shit.
You should stay in today,
amateur. Creampie, internal breeding:
you can watch, but you can't."

The Summer before the Student Murders

Florida, 1990

Persian Gulf
Persian rugs
Gimme golf
Give me drugs

Psycho House
Walkabout
Mickey Mouse
Pulling out

Take a load
Take a loss
Mr. Toad
Who's the boss

Pitch a tent
Boy in blue
Boy for rent
Overdue

Sandy trap
Going rogue
Jockey strap
Come on vogue

Lie awake
Twist the knob
Turkey Lake
Gobble gob

Chippendale
Chicken fight
Killer whale
Killer night

Long Beach

Ralph W. Mann, 1909–1982

Was it one,
was it two
families
he had walked
out on before
the affair
with my grandmother
Ora?
Lies
no one knew.
No one talked

His father,
William,
sheriff and engineer,
was a semipro
failure
with the San Pedro
Pilots,
where he played
with the great,
hated
Babe Ruth.

William
banned
his son
from sport—
punishment
of a sort.
Grandpa
dropped
out of USC,
with his friend
Marion Morrison,

for baseball.
William
pointed
a Remington
at him,
the shortened
barrel.
Grandpa's Mexican
mother
in the background,
never mentioned.

His pitching arm
was just short
of enough.
But he was strong;
this was Long
Beach:
he worked
his way up
to supervisor
of Crescent Wharf
and Warehouse.

There were three
types of men:
loaders
as the pallet
came in,
jitney drivers,
and the guys
who played cards
and pulled the boards
out from under
the crane.

He didn't go
to WWII:
he ran the docks.

Tick, tock.
At a strike,
union men
on his left
and right
got shot.
The higher-ups
looking down.

He retired
as supervisor,
nowhere to go.
Enraged
at change,
alcoholic,
with a pension
for life.
Not to mention
a wife
to overlook.

In 1975,
the Shah
brought
him to Iran
to organize a port.
He felt
half alive.
He thought
like an engineer—
better than one—
but wasn't paid

like an engineer,
which helped everyone
but him. He barely
made it
out, before
the Revolution.

A few coins,
the dictator
in his pocket.
He showed me
on a visit.

He spent
his last years
as a volunteer
umpire,
youth baseball.
Behind a mask.
Ask
what he meant.
Dying horribly
of esophageal
cancer,

in Long Beach.

Beginning & Ending with a Line by Michelle Boisseau

1955–2017

What kind of end of the world is this,
with no new poems from you?
Night arrives too early in November:
clocks turn back; the light dims.

We met in class, in Tennessee.
Nothing can be rewritten, but I remember how
you gave me changes, and I changed.
You kept going, for twenty years.

I'm not fighting, so much as absorbing,
you said, the last time we talked.
I want to write, but the metaphors won't come.
I don't have a way to even talk about this.

I don't have a way to even talk about this.
I want to write, but the metaphors won't come,
you said, the last time we talked.
I'm not fighting, so much as absorbing.

You kept going. For twenty years
you gave me changes, and I changed.
Nothing can be rewritten. But I remember how
we met, in class, in Tennessee.

Clocks, turn back. The light dims:
night arrives, too early in November,
with no new poems from you.
What kind of end of the world is this.

Playboy

Much was offered, it turns out, in 1978.
Men in ads were in no way confused:
they wanted the girl on the cover
of the May *Playboy*.
Inside, Anita Bryant railed against homosexual
teachers, took it to the soft-core street.

She was the bane of Castro Street.
The Sunshine Girl of 1978.
"We call him a fruit, the homosexual:
eater of sperm, God's forbidden fruit." Confused?
The filthiest piece in *Playboy*,
her words made the cover;

her career didn't recover.
Something was stirring in the street
nothing to do with *Playboy*—
nothing and everything, in 1978:
a pretty flag; another assassination. Not to be confused:
no self-respecting homosexual

says *homosexual*. But teachers are still undercover,
and people confuse us with pedophiles on Main Street.
It's always 1978 in the pages of *Playboy*.

A New Syntax

1

This is the arrangement:
polo shirts, white-collar crime.
The letters refuse to add up.
They say it's early days.

Polo shirts: white-collar crime
against fashion, and the rest of us.
They say it's early days,
just to level-set.

Against fashion, and the rest of us,
trends turn from cold to civil,
just to level-set.
Get a life. Style

trends turn from cold to civil.
Press the button:
get a lifestyle,
like a cup of alphabet soup.

Press the button.
This is the arrangement.
Like a cup of alphabet soup,
the letters refuse to add up.

2

The letters refuse to add up,
to mark my place.
The neighbors hissed,
What are you?

to mark my place.
In other words.
What are you?
They called me *yellow* in Lexington.

In other words,
I have a stock response.
They called me yellow in Lexington
when I was a little boy.

I have a stock response;
the percentages are rough.
When I was a little boy,
the bluegrass was something else.

The percentages are rough.
The letters refuse to add up;
the bluegrass was. *Something else,*
the neighbors hissed.

3

The neighbors hissed
in the post-election daze.
Like a lover,
I spent the night at Blow Buddies.

In the post-election daze,
the deejay spun "Last Christmas."
I spent the night at Blow Buddies,
which is one too many.

The deejay spun "Last Christmas."
George Michael was news again,
which is one too many
poster boys of childhood gone.

George Michael was news. Again,
I woke up on Christmas.
Poster boys of childhood gone.
My god, I thought you were someone to rely on.

I woke up on Christmas.
The neighbors hissed,
My god, I thought you were someone to rely on,
like a lover.

4

Like a lover,
maybe we're all running.
This is the arrangement,
in terms of next steps.

Maybe. We're all running.
This is our cell-fate.
In terms of next steps,
it's only summer.

This is our cell-fate.
The phones of the dead chirp.
It's only summer—
the ban had been; storms come later.

The phones of the dead chirp.
A monument falls in the night.
The ban had been; storms come later.
The California wildflowers . . .

A monument falls in the night,
like a lover.
The California wildflowers.
This is the arrangement.

Notes

The first section's epigraph comes from Bill Knott's "Humidity's Tones."

"In the Beginning": The epigraph is from Laura Jensen's "There Was a Woman."

"Deal": The epigraph is the entirety of Ed Smith's "Converse All Stars."

"In the Rapid Autumn of Libraries": The title phrase comes from Italo Calvino's *If on a winter's night a traveler.*

"Wi-Fi": The structure of this poem is informed by Karl Tierney's "Arkansas Landscape: Wish You Were Here" and "June 21, 1989."

"One-Night Stand": The epigraph is from David Trinidad's "Night and Fog."

"Poem Beginning with a Line by Wayne Koestenbaum": The line was a tweet sent by Koestenbaum on November 28, 2021.

"Against Metaphor": The epigraph is from Alfred Starr Hamilton's "Gold Standard."

"The Turn of the Year": The poem is after Donald Justice's "The Thin Man."

"The Shortened History of Florida": This poem is after Jamie McKendrick's "A Shortened History in Pictures."

"The End of the Last Summer": The last line is taken from Wilfred Owen's "To ——."

"Cockroach": "Calvins" are Calvin Klein jeans. "Mr. Roboto" is a reference to the Styx song of the same name.

"September Elegies": This poem is in memory of Seth Walsh, Justin Aaberg, Billy Lucas, and Tyler Clementi, bullied gay kids who committed suicide.

"Larkin Street": The phrase "pretending to be me" comes from Philip Larkin's "An Interview with the *Observer*," which was collected in Larkin's *Required Writing: Miscellaneous Pieces 1955–1982*.

"Teaser": *Hustler White* is a Bruce LaBruce film starring Tony Ward.

"Untoward Occurrence at Embassy Suites Poetry Reading": This poem is after Marilyn Hacker's "Untoward Occurrence at Embassy Poetry Reading."

"Nothing": The quoted line is from Czesław Miłosz's "Should, Should Not."

"Realtor": "House in Vermont" and "high five" are slang for HIV.

"Halston": A few details are taken from *Simply Halston* by Steven Gaines.

"A Better Life": This poem is after "Policronías" by Julio Cortázar.

"Florida Again": The epigraph and formal structure of the poem come from "Talbot Road" by Thom Gunn.

"*Everybody Everybody*": "Everybody Everybody" was a song released in 1990 by the band Black Box, which was seemingly fronted by the model Katrin Quinol. In truth, she lip-synced in the video; the singer was Martha Wash.

"Weather": The epigraph is from Donald Britton's poem "Serenade."

"Long Beach": Marion Morrison is the birth name of John Wayne.

"Beginning & Ending with a Line by Michelle Boisseau": The line is from Michelle's poem "Verge."

About the Author

A queer poet, critic, and medical writer, Randall Mann is the author of five previous poetry collections: *Complaint in the Garden, Breakfast with Thom Gunn, Straight Razor, Proprietary,* and *A Better Life.* He is also the author of a book of criticism, essays, and interviews, *The Illusion of Intimacy: On Poetry.* His writing has appeared in *The Adroit Journal, Kenyon Review, Literary Hub, The Paris Review, Poetry, San Francisco Chronicle,* and elsewhere. He is the recipient of the Kenyon Review Prize in Poetry and the J. Howard and Barbara M.J. Wood Prize from *Poetry,* and his books have been shortlisted for the Lambda Literary Award, California Book Award, and Northern California Book Award. Mann lives in San Francisco.

Poetry is vital to language and living. Since 1972, Copper Canyon Press has published extraordinary poetry from around the world to engage the imaginations and intellects of readers, writers, booksellers, librarians, teachers, students, and donors.

WE ARE GRATEFUL FOR THE MAJOR SUPPORT PROVIDED BY:

academy of american poets

THE PAUL G. ALLEN
FAMILY FOUNDATION

amazon literary partnership

4
CULTURE

the point
envision·enact·evolve

Lannan

ART WORKS.
National
Endowment
for the Arts
arts.gov

WASHINGTON STATE
ARTS COMMISSION

A&
OFFICE OF ARTS & CULTURE
SEATTLE

The Witter Bynner Foundation
for Poetry

TO LEARN MORE ABOUT UNDERWRITING
COPPER CANYON PRESS TITLES,
PLEASE CALL 360-385-4925 EXT. 103

WE ARE GRATEFUL FOR THE MAJOR SUPPORT PROVIDED BY:

Richard Andrews and Colleen
   Chartier
Anonymous
Jill Baker and Jeffrey Bishop
Anne and Geoffrey Barker
Donna Bellew
Matthew Bellew
Sarah Bird
Will Blythe
John Branch
Diana Broze
Sarah Cavanaugh
Keith Cowan and Linda Walsh
Stephanie Ellis-Smith and
   Douglas Smith
Mimi Gardner Gates
Gull Industries Inc. on behalf of
   William True
The Trust of Warren A. Gummow
William R. Hearst III
Carolyn and Robert Hedin
David and Jane Hibbard
Bruce S. Kahn
Phil Kovacevich and Eric Wechsler
Lakeside Industries Inc. on behalf
   of Jeanne Marie Lee

Maureen Lee and Mark Busto
Peter Lewis and Johanna Turiano
Ellie Mathews and Carl Youngmann
   as The North Press
Larry Mawby and Lois Bahle
Hank and Liesel Meijer
Jack Nicholson
Petunia Charitable Fund and
   adviser Elizabeth Hebert
Madelyn Pitts
Suzanne Rapp and Mark Hamilton
Adam and Lynn Rauch
Emily and Dan Raymond
Joseph C. Roberts
Jill and Bill Ruckelshaus
Cynthia Sears
Kim and Jeff Seely
Nora Hutton Shepard
D.D. Wigley
Joan F. Woods
Barbara and Charles Wright
In honor of C.D. Wright,
   from Forrest Gander
Caleb Young as C. Young Creative
The dedicated interns and faithful
   volunteers of Copper Canyon Press

The pressmark for Copper Canyon Press
suggests entrance, connection, and interaction
while holding at its center
an attentive, dynamic space for poetry.

This book is set in Minion Pro.
Book design by Phil Kovacevich.
Printed on archival-quality paper.